Ghost Writer

A Play for Young People

N. J. Warburton

Samuel French – London
New York – Sydney – Toronto – Hollywood

Please see page vi for further copyright information.

CHARACTERS

Jeffrey
Belinda
Mrs Spruce
Colonel
Butler
Vicar
Maid
Colonel's wife
Her cousin
Ghost
Director
Cashflow
Arnold
Policeman
Ron
Mavis
Edwin
Vera
King
Queen
Messenger
Convicts
Policemen

The action of the play takes place in the writers' study, and the Colonel's lounge.

Time—the present

AUTHOR'S NOTE

The cast is large but many of the parts can be doubled. Most can also be either male or female. There can be as many or as few pirates, policemen, etc. as resources allow. The set should be simple but needs to suggest both the writers' study and the Colonel's lounge.

N. J. Warburton

Other one-act plays by N. J. Warburton,
published by Samuel French Ltd:

Don't Blame It on the Boots
Receive This Light
Sour Grapes and Ashes
Zartan

COPYRIGHT INFORMATION
(See also page ii)

GHOST WRITER

A study

Jeffrey and Belinda are writing a thriller, one typing, the other standing in thought. The last word is typed

Jeffrey There. What do you think?

Belinda Yes. It's got something. It's definitely going to work.

Jeffrey I think we've got to do something special with the murder. I mean the murder's the key bit . . .

Belinda Quite. If the murder's right the rest will just fall into place.

Jeffrey Let's give it five minutes of concentrated thought, then, shall we?

Belinda Good idea. Five minutes, in total silence. See if we can stir the muse.

They go into deep thought

> *Mrs Spruce enters with mop and bucket*

Spruce (*singing*) "Some day my prince will come . . ."

Belinda Mrs Spruce! Mrs Spruce, what are you doing?

Spruce Just giving the room a bit of a tidy. Can't work in a mucky room, can you?

Jeffrey But . . . can't you see we're writing?

Spruce Ooh, fancy. But don't worry your heads about that; it won't bother me. (*Singing*) "Some day my prince will come . . ."

Jeffrey Mrs Spruce! Mrs Spruce!

Spruce Yes?

Belinda You don't seem to realize: we need quiet.

Spruce Quiet?

Jeffrey Yes. We've just got the murder to do.

Spruce The murder? Oo-er.

Jeffrey And all this row is *very* annoying.

Spruce (*backing away*) Look. I'm ever so sorry about the singing. I can't help it, you see. It's my disposition.

Belinda (*taking a step towards her*) You do understand . . .

Spruce (*holding up the mop*) Ow! Keep off me. Keep your distance.

Belinda Mrs Spruce ...
Spruce My son goes to karate, you know.
Jeffrey (*shouting*) Mrs Spruce!
Spruce Ow!!

She runs off

Jeffrey Stupid woman.
Belinda (*calling after her*) We were *writing* a murder, Mrs Spruce, not committing one.
Jeffrey Oh, let her go. She'll be back.
Belinda Are you sure?
Jeffrey She came back when we were writing the one about the blood-sucking alien, didn't she? Come on, let's get on with the play.
Belinda I suppose you're right. Where were we, then?
Jeffrey Er ... (*Reading from the typewriter*) "The Colonel enters from the right ..."

A Colonel enters. From now on the action on stage mirrors their writing

He sits at the writing-desk

The Colonel does so

Belinda No. Better make that the sofa.

The Colonel moves to the sofa

The Butler and the Vicar enter from the right.

The Butler and the Vicar enter from R

Jeffrey The Butler announces the Vicar.
Butler The Reverend Smith to see you, sir.
Belinda You can't just say that. You have to say his first name too.
Butler The Reverend Wayne Smith to see you, sir.
Jeffrey No.
Butler The Reverend Wayne Blenkinsop to——
Belinda No, no. Not quite ...
Butler The Vicar to see you, sir.
Vicar (*in a high-pitched voice*) You asked me to call, Colonel!
Belinda Says the Vicar in a deep and fruity voice.

Vicar (*in a deep, fruity voice*) You asked me to call, Colonel?
Colonel Ah, Vicar. Good to see you.
Jeffrey Says the Colonel, standing.

The Colonel stands

Belinda No, still seated. He's rather pompous, remember.

The Colonel sits

Jeffrey Yes, but he's feeling the pangs of guilt.

The Colonel stands

Belinda Do you really think so?

The Colonel is about to sit

Jeffrey Definitely.
Colonel (*aside*) Make your minds up. (*To the Vicar*) The fact is, Vicar, I've got a bit of a confession to make. You see, a long time ago I did something that was really rather naughty.
Belinda We can't say naughty.
Colonel Bad.
Jeffrey No.
Colonel Diabolical.
Belinda Wicked, I think.
Colonel Sure?
Belinda Yes. Wicked.
Colonel Wicked.
Vicar I can't imagine you ever doing anything wicked, Colonel.
Colonel Well, I can assure you I did and it's about time I got it off my chest ...
Belinda Yes, this is all right. Let's skip through to the point of the murder.

As Belinda and Jeffrey flick through the script, the characters move and speak (rhubarbs only) at double speed

Colonel (*confessing*) Rhubarb, rhubarb, rhubarbrhubarb rhubarb.
Vicar (*shocked*) Rhubarb rhubarb!

They argue fiercely (in rhubarbs)

   The Vicar storms out

The Colonel puts his head in his hands and sobs

Butler (*comforting*) Rhubarb rhubarb, sir.
Colonel (*snapping*) Rhubarb!

The Butler hurries out as the Maid comes in with the Colonel's wife and her cousin, Clarissa. Rhubarbed greetings are exchanged

Colonel (*asking the time*) Rhubarb rhubarbrhubarb?
Maid (*shaking her watch and listening to it*) Rhubarb rhubarbrhubarb, sir.
Colonel (*angrily*) Rhubarb rhubarb! Rhubarb rhubarbrhubarb!

The Maid flees, sobbing

There is another fierce argument and the Colonel sends the others out

The Colonel's wife and her cousin exit. The Butler creeps back in and is about to shoot the Colonel when ...

Jeffrey Stop. Here we are. Just turn back to the bit where the Colonel throws the ladies out.

Belinda turns back some pages

The Butler creeps out backwards. The Colonel's wife and her cousin run backwards

Belinda That's it. From there.
Colonel (*angrily, at normal speed*) Leave me in peace, all of you! You may go and pack, Clarissa. I shall throw you out in the morning.
Clarissa Where has this cruel streak come from, Nigel?
Colonel Enough! Leave me!

The ladies run off, sobbing. The Butler creeps on, as before, but this time shoots the Colonel who dies

Jeffrey Perfect. The mystery is now set up.
Belinda Who killed the guilty Colonel?
Ghost (*off*) The Butler did it!
Belinda What? Who said that?
Ghost (*off, approaching*) I did.
Jeffrey And how, pray, did you work that out?

The Ghost enters

Ghost That's just it. I didn't work it out. I didn't have to.

Belinda What?

Ghost I could see. The Butler actually came on. Everyone could see him. You can't bring your murderer on if you want it to be a secret. You should disguise him or keep him off stage. Some of my best murders took place off stage.

Jeffrey Your murders?

Ghost Yes. I've bumped off the best of them in my time, you know. Kings, queens. All the nobility. Great stuff.

Belinda As a murderer, you mean?

Ghost No, as a writer.

Jeffrey Ah, you're a writer.

Ghost Of course. Well, I was. I haven't actually put pen to paper in, oh, more than three hundred years.

Belinda Three hundred?

Jeffrey But you can't. I mean, it's not possible. I mean. you'd be . . .

Belinda You'd be dead.

Ghost That's right. And so I am. Technically, anyway. I used to do a lot, though. You may have seen some. Bags of bodies I had in some of them. Well, I ought to be off, I suppose. Shouldn't have butted in really; it's just that, well, when there's a play in the offing I find it hard to keep quiet. You know how it is.

Jeffrey Oh yes. Quite.

Ghost Well . . . (*He bows and makes to leave*)

Belinda No, don't go.

Ghost Yes?

Belinda Perhaps you could stay and——

Jeffrey —lend us a hand.

Ghost I don't know. I'm not really supposed to, you know.

Jeffrey But, you see, we're not actually sure how all this will end . . .

Ghost Of course not. It's not up to you in any case.

Belinda Not up to us?

Ghost No. Look, it takes a lot of people to put a play on. Not just the writers. I mean, there's the director.

Jeffrey The director?

Ghost Of course. They're full of ideas, directors are. Here, I'll show you. (*He waves an arm*)

The Director enters, clapping

Director All right, everyone. On stage please. Come along, dar-
lings, shift yourselves!

The Colonel gets up

  The rest of the cast join him on stage

Director Now, this is the way I see the play. What it's really about
is thwarted love ...
Belinda No it isn't.
Director It's obvious to me that the Maid and the Vicar are
secretly in love and the Colonel's wife has this thing going for
Clarissa ...
Jeffrey What's he talking about?
Ghost Just watch. You may learn something.
Butler Excuse me but where does it say all this?
Jeffrey Quite.
Director It doesn't actually *say* it. It's in the sub-text.
Butler The what?
Director The sub-text, darling, the sub-text. Don't they teach you
people anything these days? Right, let's go back to the begin-
ning, shall we? And this time play it for romance. OK? All right,
places everyone. Act one, scene one, enter the Butler with the
Vicar.

The Colonel remains while ...

  The other actors clear the stage

  The Butler enters

Butler The Vicar to see you, sir.

  *The Vicar enters with the Maid clinging to his legs and looking
  imploringly at him. Unseen by the Colonel, he pulls the Maid to
  her feet and falls to his knees to adore her. The Maid backs out
  blowing kisses*

Vicar You asked me to call, Colonel?
Jeffrey Stop! We didn't write this. Get them off our stage.

With a gesture the Ghost stops the action

  The Director exits

Ghost I told you. It's not just your play. Other people have their ideas too.

Belinda Yes but that was a completely *different* play ...

Ghost It's only the start, my dear. The director isn't the only one who likes to dabble ...

Another gesture brings on Cashflow, a richly dressed figure with a cigar. He is followed by Arnold, an assistant with a clipboard

Jeffrey Who's this?

Ghost He's the man who's putting up the money.

Cashflow OK, relax everybody. Just popped in to see how the play was going.

Arnold Relax, everyone. Come along. Let's see you all relaxing.

Cashflow What do you think, Arnold?

Arnold What do I think, Mr Cashflow?

Cashflow Yeah, what do you think?

Arnold It's ... well ... what's the word?

Cashflow Slow.

Arnold Slow. That's it. You're so right, Mr Cashflow. Slow, slow, slow. (*To the cast*) I wish you people would appreciate the need to speed things up!

Cashflow Exactly, Arnold. Too much talk. People don't go to the theatre for talk. You can get talk on a bus.

Arnold (*a hearty laugh*) Of course you can. (*To the cast*) You're talking too much, do you understand?

Cashflow What people come to see is music.

Arnold Music! Soaring strings, swelling sounds! Yes, yes. A huge orchestra playing non-stop ...

Cashflow Wait a minute, wait a minute. We ain't paying for no orchestra. People come to see music or they come to see fights.

Arnold Of course they do. Where's the aggression? Where's the fights?

Cashflow It needs some spicing up. Let me see, let me see.

He paces, with Arnold in support

Cashflow I've got it, I've got it. This old guy lives on the edge of the moors, right?

Arnold Right, right.

Cashflow And on the night of the murder there's a prison break-out——

Arnold —from the local prison. Great idea, Mr Cashflow.

Cashflow —and all these convicts hole up here for the night.

Arnold Brilliant! Absolutely brilliant. It's the perfect touch. Well, come on, everybody. Let's see what it looks like. Let's have some action. (*He claps his hands*)

The Maid enters

Colonel What time is it, Mabel?

The Maid shakes her watch and listens to it

> *Meanwhile a number of Convicts burst in, unnoticed, followed by several Policemen. There is a shoot-out and some hand-to-hand fighting before they all exit*

Maid I'm afraid my watch has stopped, sir.

Colonel What? I don't pay you to keep a faulty watch. If you can't wear a decent watch then you'd better look elsewhere for employment. Consider yourself fired!

Cashflow That's more like it. Arnold, get the director to write that in.

He exits, followed by Arnold

Arnold (*as he goes*) Great. Really great. Just what this show needed. I don't know how you do it, Mr Cashflow. You have such a subtle touch. I was wondering if I might clean your car during lunch, Mr Cashflow. May I? Please?

Belinda But that ruined it. Who were all those people?

Ghost They were to bring the audiences in. If that's what people want that's what you have to write. Or so Mr Cashflow says.

Jeffrey But it didn't make sense.

Ghost It did to Mr Cashflow. If Mr Cashflow wanted to use a dozen one-legged pirates carrying hot-water bottles he'd put them in . . .

The Butler enters and coughs

Butler Excuse me, sir. There are twelve uniped naval gentlemen at the door, sir, each with a——

Jeffrey Stop it! We haven't put that in. Yet.

Ghost No, I don't suppose I'd agree to that myself. But you still have to remember that you must write a play that people want to see.

Belinda But if we do that, it should be all right then, shouldn't it?
Ghost (*doubtfully*) Well ...
Jeffrey But what else could go wrong?
Ghost The actors.
Belinda The actors? How can they muck things up? They only have to say the lines, don't they?
Ghost With feeling, though. Let's see. Have you got a bit where the policeman is shown the body? There's usually a bit like that.
Jeffrey We have, as a matter of fact.
Ghost (*with a gesture*) We'll have a look at that, then.

The Butler and the Maid exit

The Colonel resumes the dead position

The Maid enters with a Policeman

Maid (*choking slightly*) This is where we found him, sergeant.
Policeman (*with a slight start*) Good heavens.
Jeffrey But what's wrong with that? That's what we wrote.
Ghost Ah yes. But now watch them do the same bit with the same words, only this time with feeling. (*He gestures*)

The Maid and the Policeman exit and enter. The Maid is sobbing uncontrollably

Maid This ... this is where ... we found him ... (*She flings herself down, weeping*)
Policeman (*staggering back with shock and revulsion*) Good heavens!! (*He is sick in his helmet*)
Colonel (*reviving*) I'm not quite ... dead ...
Jeffrey That's enough! You are dead. Now get off, all of you! (*He chases them off*)

The Colonel, the Maid and the Policeman exit

Ghost There you are, you see. There's more to putting on a play than just writing the words. The actors alone make sure it's a different play every time it's done.
Belinda But, surely, if everyone tries hard to get every detail right ...
Jeffrey And if we make sure no-one ruins it all ...
Ghost Then it can still go wrong.
Jeffrey But how? How?

Ghost The audience. (*He gestures*)

Ron and Mavis enter to take their seats in the auditorium

You can't do it without them, you know.

Mavis Ron, Ron! I think they've started.

Ron I could've told you that, woman. We got the wrong bus in the first place. I said, didn't I, change at *The Baker's Arms?* But would you listen? No, you would not.

Mavis Don't start on at me, Ron. It was your idea in the first place. I'd've been quite happy with the telly. I suppose you know what we're missing.

Ron Stop talking rubbish, woman. This is all live, isn't it? Now get to your seat.

They sit next to two other members of the audience, Edwin and Vera

Have we missed much? Only Mavis insisted we should get on the wrong bus. Changed at *The King's Head* instead of——

Edwin Sssh!

Ron Pardon?

Edwin I said "sssh!"

Vera Edwin! Will you be quiet?

Edwin Me? I was just telling this person to be quiet.

Vera Well don't make so much noise about it.

Mavis Sssh! Keep your voices down.

Vera I beg your pardon?

Mavis They're about to start. Keep your noise to yourselves.

Vera Well, of all the——

The Colonel enters as for the start of the play

Ron Oh look. It's him.

Mavis Him? Who's him when he's at home?

Ron You know. What's-his-name? In that thing, on telly . . .

Mavis Jack'll Fix It?

Ron Who?

Mavis You know, the one with the hair. Jack'll Fix It, or Do It or something . . .

Vera Jim, you mean.

Mavis Jim? Is that who it is?

Edwin Sssh!

Vera No, it's Jim'll Fix It not Jack but this isn't him.

Ron No, no. It was the thing with all those pirates in. Daft thing, it was ...

Edwin I know. Where they had these hot-water bottles ...

Ron That's the one. What's it called now?

Mavis Panorama?

Ron Panorama? Use your head, woman.

Vera Blue Peter?

Edwin No, Vera. Blue Peter's the one with the donkey. Oh isn't it awful? It's on the tip of my tongue ...

Colonel It was the South Bank Show ...

Ron
Mavis (*together*) The South Bank Show! Of course!
Vera
Edwin

The Butler enters

Mavis (*sharing out crisps, etc.*) Ooh, he's nice. Nice and polite.

The Butler bows towards Mavis

Butler The Vicar to see you, sir.

Mavis Ooh, a vicar. Fancy.

Vera I might. Depends on the vicar.

They laugh loudly as ...

The Vicar enters

Ron Now, I've seen him somewhere before as well ...

Edwin So have I, only I thought he was dead ...

Jeffrey I can't stand any more of this! Get out, go on. Go home and watch the telly.

He drives them out

Belinda And take your picnic with you!

Jeffrey enters

Jeffrey That's it. That's the last straw. I'm packing it all in.

Ghost Cheer up. You should see what they've done to some of my stuff over the years.

Belinda Don't give up, Jeffrey. We could start again; make a better job of it.

Jeffrey But the play's stuffed with characters we didn't invent. How are we going to get rid of them?

Ghost That's no problem. Write them out.

Jeffrey Write them out?

Ghost Yes. I'll show you. (*He sits at the typewriter and sets it aside, taking up a quill*) Do you mind if I use one of these? I could never get on with machinery. Now then. A touch of the old blank verse, I think. (*He writes*)

A King and Queen appear

Ah, this is more like it. I love these bits.

Belinda But that's two *more* characters. I thought you were supposed to be getting rid of people.

Ghost Wait and see.

King Grave tidings, sweet.

Queen   Much though it troubles me
I must attend. What news, my Lord? Say on.

King That worthy dame with brush and spray and pan,
            One Mistress Spruce —

Queen   I know the noble wench!

King Noble, indeed. Her way she made unto
            The whelk stand that tops the cliff at Dover
            When twelve stout knaves did set upon her there.

Queen Ah, me! Poor lady.

King   Pirates were they all
            With but the dozen legs to walk withal.

Queen Then did she struggle with them?

King   Ay, right well.
            With her fierce broom all twelve she did dispatch,
            Sweeping them bravely off the cliff.

Queen   What dead?
            Are all the pirates dead?

King   Ay, dead and gone.
            She to her death did plummet with them all;
            Also a band of pris'ners on the run
            Passing at the time did fall!

Queen   Oh, woe! Woe!

A Messenger enters, dropping on one knee

Ghost Now a dash of prose, I think.

Messenger Sad tidings, my Lord.

King Speak on, man.

Messenger My lords Ron and Edwin with their good ladies, whilst partaking of a picnic with some theatrical people atop the cliffs at Dover . . .

Queen No! It cannot be!

Messenger 'Tis so, my Lady. All, all washed out to sea . . .

King The tears start to my eyes. Were all the players lost?

Messenger No, good my Lord. The Maid and Butler have survived this sorry event.

Queen Then here is some relief.

Messenger I fear it is but scant relief, my Lady. The Butler did accuse the Maid, saying it was her rotten watch that did cause them all to miss the turning of the tide. The Maid in anger hath called the Butler to fight a duel. Here they come now.

The Maid and the Butler enter, attended. They fight

The Butler accidentally runs the Queen through and stands back aghast

Butler This poison shall repay me for my sin.
          My Queen I've killed and therefore I must die. (*He drinks the poison and dies*)

King Foul maid! All this is caused by thy bad watch!

He falls upon the Maid. They struggle and are both killed

Messenger How these dark deeds do tell against my age!
          My poor heart doth break to see so many die. (*He falls down in a faint*)

Ghost There you are! That's cleared the decks a bit. You must admit, they don't write plays like that these days.

Jeffrey But . . .

Belinda But . . .

Ghost Ah yes. One last touch. (*He resumes writing*)

Belinda Look at it. Look at it. Bodies all over the place.

Jeffrey Well, don't blame me. It was your idea to write a thriller in the first place.

Belinda You suggested it. You said we'd make a bomb.

Jeffrey I would've done. By myself.

Belinda Oh, so it's my fault, is it?

Jeffrey You've always held me back. I was the one with the talent.
Belinda You swine, Jeffrey!

She snatches the gun from the Butler's pocket and shoots Jeffrey who staggers, grabs a dagger and stabs her. They both fall

Ghost (*adding the final full stop*) There! That's what I call an ending!

CURTAIN

FURNITURE AND PROPERTY LIST

Only essential items of furniture as mentioned in the text are listed below.
Further dressing may be added at the director's discretion.

On stage: *The Writers' study*
Desk. *On it:* typewriter, paper, script, quills
Chair

The Colonel's lounge
Writing desk
Sofa

Off stage: Mop and bucket **(Mrs Spruce)**
Gun **(Butler)**
Cigar **(Cashflow)**
Clipboard **(Arnold)**
Guns **(Policemen)**
Packet of crisps **(Mavis)**
Dagger **(King)**
Swords **(Butler, Maid)**

Personal: **Maid:** wrist-watch (required throughout)
Butler: phial of poison, gun (in pocket)

LIGHTING PLOT

Practical fittings required: *nil*

Interior. The same scene throughout

No cues

EFFECTS PLOT

No cues